Also by Daniel Halpern

SOMETHING SHINING

Something Shining

POEMS BY

DANIEL HALPERN

ALFRED A. KNOPF · NEW YORK

2001

THIS IS A BORZOI BOOK
PUBLISHED BY ALFRED A. KNOPF

Library of Congress Cataloguing-in-Publication Data
Halpern, Daniel, [date]
Something shining : new poems / Daniel Halpern
p.   cm.
ISBN 0-375-40733-2 / PBK. 0-375-70720-4
I. Title.
PS3558.A397S66   1999
811'.54—dc21
99-15601
CIP

Manufactured in the United States of America
Published November 16, 1999
First Paperback Edition, April 2001

"My Eyes Your Eyes" is for Lily, "Thaw" is for Henry, "All City" is
for Frank, "A Bad Year" is for Laurie, "Rusted Tin" is for Russ,
"The Eternal Light of Talk" is for Bill, "In Season" is for Richard,
and "Measures She Has Taken" borrows an image from Rimbaud.

AS ALWAYS,
FOR JEANNE & LILY

The definition of beauty is easy;
it is what leads to desperation.

— PAUL VALÉRY

CONTENTS

SOMETHING SHINING

ZENO'S LEMUR

Isn't he the man with crimson socks
    and the slow loris climbing
        like the hour hand from his shoulder,
    over his ear and up
to the pale dome of his head?

The man's face shines with affection.
    He's an honest man and his pet,
        lackadaisical but not dispassionate,
    is devoted and clear about the nature
of their relationship. There are times

to eat and times to climb, the two things
    a loris is always in the act of.
        As the man turns, nearly in slow motion,
    the slow loris peers
from behind his left ear and a smile

begins to spread like a sunrise
    on his face. A word
        takes shape in his mouth as his hands
    reach into the air — reach out
as the word moves forward,

a word of arrival, recognition hovering before him.

HER BODY

The Fingers

They are small enough to find and care for a tiny stone.
    To lift it with wobbly concentration from the ground,
        from the family of stones, up past the pursed mouth —

for this we are thankful — to a place level with her eyes
    to take a close look, a look into the nature of stone.
        Like everything, it is for the first time: first stone,

chilly cube of ice, soft rise of warm flesh, hard
    surface of table leg, first and lasting scent of grass
        rubbed between the tiny pincer fingers. And there is

the smallest finger poking the air, pointing toward the first heat
    of the single sun, pointing toward the friendly angels
        who sent her, letting them know contact's made.

The Eyes

We believe their color makes some kind of difference,
the cast of it played off the color of hair and face.

But it makes no difference, blue or brown,
hazel, green, or gray, pale sky or sand.

When sleep-burdened they'll turn up into her,
close back down upon her sizable will.

But when she's ready for the yet-to-come —
oh, they widen, grow a deep cool sheen

to catch the available light and shine
with the intensity of the newly arrived.

If they find you they'll hold on relentlessly
without guile, the gaze no less than interrogatory,

fixed, immediate, bringing to bear what there's been
to date. Call her name and perhaps they'll turn to you,

or they might be engaged, looking deeply into the nature
of other things—the affect of wall, the texture of rug,

into something very small that's fallen to the floor
and needs to be isolated and controlled. Maybe

an afternoon reflection, an insect moving *slowly,*
maybe just looking with loyalty into the eyes of another.

The Toes

Who went to market?
Who stayed home?
This one goes,
this one doesn't.
This one eats

the flesh
of grass-eating mammals,
this one does not.
In the 17th century
Bashō—delicate master

of the vagaries of who
went where—
wrote to one he loved

not of market
and not of meat

but something brief,
abbreviated,
like five unburdened toes
fluttering like cilia
in the joy of a drafty room —

    You go,
  I stay.
    Two autumns.

The Signature

Who knows how they get here,
beyond the obvious.
Who packaged the code

that provided the slate for her eyes,
and what about the workmanship
that went into the fingers,

allowing such intricate movement
just months from the other side? —
Who placed with such exactness

the minute nails on each
of the ten unpainted toes?
And what remains

beyond eye and ear, the thing
most deeply rooted in her body —
the thing that endlessly blossoms

but doesn't age, in time
shows greater vitality? The thing
unlike the body that so quickly

reaches its highest moment only
to begin, with little hesitation,
the long roll back, slowing all the way

until movement is administered
by devices other than those devised
by divine design. The ageless thing

without a name, like air, both resident
and owner of the body's estate.
But this thing, only partially

unpackaged, sings
through the slate that guards it,
contacts those of us waiting here

with a splay of its soft,
scrutinizing fingers.
Her spirit is a sapling thing,

something green, still damp
but resolute, entering this world
with an angel's thumb pressed

to her unformed body at the very last,
a template affixed to her body
when they decided it was time

to let her go, for her to come to us
and their good work was done.
An angel's thumbprint, a signature.

AFTER THE VIGIL

They turn up, no longer nameless,
their bodies clear, so nearly pure
they appear in morning light transparent.

They turn up and one day look at you
for the first time, their eyes sure now
you are one of theirs, surely here to stay.

They turn up wearing an expression of yours,
imitating your mouth, the smile perfected
over years of enduring amusing moments.

They turn up without a past, their fingers,
inexact instruments that examine what carpets
their turf, what they inherit through blood.

They turn up with your future, if not in mind
very much in the explosive story of their genes,
in gesture foreshadowing the what's-to-come.

They turn up with your hair—albeit not much
of it—something in the color, the curl of it
after the bath, its bearing after sleep.

They turn up already on their own, ideas
of their own, settling on their own limits,
their particular sense of things.

They turn up and we have been waiting,
as they have without knowing. They turn
into this world, keeping their own counsel.

TO A DAUGHTER

When we are no longer the only ones you
come home to, remember us, too.
If the infinite stars of night
end up finite in sunlight
come on home, daughter, our girl, our first light.

THE NEW ROAD

Stippled, if you were after distance.
  A layered sky, mackerel—

a mackerel sky over mackerel seas.
  The light platinum off the pines

and coastal sycamores, yellow foliage
  and mottled birch like lightning

implanted along the way. Up from the cove
  they have stripped the dead wood

and the wood still supple with sap.
  The new road begins to emerge, bare

as if newly born, raw, the brush shaved
  back, a fresh layer of dirt unearthed

for surface. And once loose, it unwinds,
  down and around, mimicking the edge

of water pressing the coast back
  to the open water of due east.

The new road displays the first to pass:
  a thin, deeply scored bicycle tire,

the mold of a child's foot placed
  to the side of a larger male shoe,

walking with intent but *patiently,* so
  exactly defined the imprint.

And for a while a small animal joined them,
  its three-pronged glyph a decoration

to the design of those walking and cycling
  the new road. Then it turns

to a promontory overlooking open ocean,
  Ragged and Pond Islands like desserts

against the vast Floridian spray of sun.
  If it's distance you're after,

this road's not for you. It turns,
  it dives, rears back, breaks and flows

a moment as if laid with a straightedge
  in cement, but finally turns

its soft dirt away from the waterline,
  up the hilly embankment toward dry land

where the new road like a wave meets the old.

MOON OVER SQUIBNOCKET

A hundred yards out The Rockpile shelters the keeper bass.
They rise from the bottom with the moon over Squibnocket
to feed on chum fish. The boats out there now
pleasure boats, boats of solitaries—captains
casting through darkness, casting for food, casting to spirits.

In a straight line the moon draws back to the beach,
cord of dimpled light white as schoolroom chalk.
We place beach chairs just beyond the tidal line
and here we sit. Shorts and T-shirts. Yet not wholly here.
Dinner of fluke and steak tips grilled rare over pale
driftwood—recent memory. A few of us sit here just looking out.
Oh yes, perfect summer night. A few of us just looking up.

KEEPERS

Judged by the inch,
those falling

short
live another day,

those beyond
the limit pay

for their sins,
if sin

is what growth is.
Greed or

subsistence, hunger
in any form

looking
for satisfaction—

something
of substance to take

home, something
whole to keep.

HOT TEA

Midafternoon.
Her canyon. Her house
a carriage house kind of,
set back

with a lot of glass
and wood stained red.
Tea brews
and the scent of Lapsang spins

from the open door with Leonard Cohen's
first album, the perfect
scent and voice
for any good year in the sixties.

She places chairs erratically
around the grass yard
and a few of us
sit down to discuss

the daily news,
a new generation
of drugs. Sunday afternoon.
She's a woman

whose boyfriends become best friends.
She still wears a dark kimono,
her hair flat black held
in a brightly colored lanyard.

She serves up wan vegetable cakes
and pale cookies from Canyon
Health. The sun
won't budge, just

another extended afternoon:
too much light. Too much time.
Too much talk waiting
for the sun to move on.

Too much water coursing
under the bridge, too many streams.
Heat from the Valley washing over us.
The tea we sip frosts our shades.

MARRIAGE POEM

Underappreciated today for his epigrammatic wit,
Ben Franklin advised in his part of the 18th century:

> *There's more to marriage*
> *than four bare legs in bed.*

A chair's been set near a stand of trees
where at night you can watch unencumbered
the heavenly configurations resolve above.
And there's time to imagine the moon,
the *moon,* made so much of
during moments of reconciliation,
introspection, and general reconsideration.

At this hour it's a shadow of itself,
a molar in the heavenly order
rounded by distance, its volume
above the chair a body of alien air,
a medium of aging light. It's best
not to name love but find a way into belief,
where *belief* like a cloudless night
reveals its interest star point by star point.

We are still four bare legs, but tonight
we've been careful to cover ourselves
with blankets—a cool night pricked
with starlight and moonlight.
It is even late at night. And here
in these chilly hours we pursue what we imagine
can be believed forever over the years.

AFTER RUMI

Nightmares fill with light like a holiday

So many nights cast to darkness
without morning.

O lovers no more, distillate sands,
body of milk flowing over.

Sun and moon, like night and day,
no longer share this room.

What you said once in the dead hour
gone without lantern through the night.

In those hours we ran to each other,
our hands towing us forward.

From one hand comes many in memory.
This was good, this despised.

But we have come to a settling,
our single direction two.

You see, so we have parted.
You see, what once was ignited

by one vision fire
no longer catches.

LOVE SONG

Your eyes the coolish pallor of the greenback

O such eyes make of what they see a cage

MY EYES YOUR EYES

I give you one of my blue eyes
Because you are four and ask for it

When we pass in the street
My blue eye looks

Between your brown eyes
And recognizes an old companion

There is a moment of envy
But it passes as we pass

Along the street
Two ships as adults like to say

Passing in the night
One a single blue beacon

The other three lights
One blue the other two

The color of soil
Holding forth

I give you one blue
And would send you another

If you asked
To improve your view of this world

If you asked
If you asked for it

FUGUE

A child asks endlessly about dying,
not death, but some fixed point,
not the state and estate of death.

It's about the invisible net
of infinity cast over
so small a frame of reference.

For the rest of us the net fills gradually in,
like an image coming up coyly but decisively
in a darkroom tray of chemicals.

We took a trip to the House of Reptiles
where I looked into the humorless eyes
of the albino reticulated python

set in the cold skull like precious, unpolished stones—
eyes like the precipice that invites
the wary to leap, pulled over by reverse phobia.

For three dollars we were allowed the chance
to face death eye to eye, inches
and a thickness of glass away,

the reptile simultaneously metaphor
and pathway out of this life,
coiled, patient, solemnly inquisitive.

Not the act of dying,
but the estate of limbo—
the days run out—no longer oneself.

DUSK

She never happens upon a garden at dusk
        doesn't wander into such magical light
        filtering through trees

the sun at so radical an angle
        its rays bent harshly across the vegetation
        carry dust from her steps as she enters

carry the million bodies of hovering sunset insects
        Her sky gray and the mist holds only
        infinite particles of water

The colors of the city chronicle black
        and white the surface of everything
        damp metal painted with drained pigment

She's not interested in relinquishing city landscape
        won't leave behind the chrome and cheerless
        The garden just beyond formalities of the city

darkens so quickly the abandoned sun remains as
        portrait in the high glass windows of the city
        a brilliant light held against the darkening below

MIDNIGHT: TRIADIC GHAZAL

Let the night be the one place of darkness.
    Water for drinking flows
        to those without appetite.

In the dark we walk through rooms
    familiar as questions
        asked of us over and over.

We know hope, light of the single star
    shed from the dying body,
        traveling, released. On its way.

Their arms outstretched. A smile
    pulling back their lips.
        Gravity. Sacrifice. Giving over

the sweet wafer of consciousness. Nails,
    straps or ropes, methods of support
        for this one portrait everlasting.

And for us the diminishing night
    if the domestic star blooms once more
        over the farthest shore.

Awake? Whatever you say.
    Part of the past is that night.
        And then, too, what lies ahead.

JUST ANOTHER DARKENING

Just a darkening, as if the century had come
to a spontaneous close, or an unexpected storm
tossed up midafternoon, the light suddenly drained
from a clear sky. A gust of wind, the thud of heavy drops
falling into the earth and the smell of earth
rich and damp—a darkness rising from the earth.

At night, waking disoriented before dawn,
the vegetation outside the window blows
to no particular rhythm. The dark out there a focus,
the night standing in for the upcoming infinity.

So sweet the scent at this hour that grows into the next
with so little speed. The light so slow to rise,
these hours so like mirrors, the night so unwilling to relinquish.

RESURRECTION

Remember the sage and wild thyme nagging their sandals,
the stones and sand underfoot the carriers
who held your body vertically and placed it
under rock to hold back the natural world.

Remember those who held you and hold you still,
walk with you in their hearts. Piero
brings you back triumphant, stick in hand
above the sleeping soldiers who guard you

if only in dream. The Artist imparts
hues of the good earth, earth of the Renaissance
to locate the moment of your reappearance.
The Poet takes you off the rock and down

into the valley with the heat of primary color,
raiment of wild flowers. And the valley
bears wild flowers that no longer
draw blood from your ankles. The poet

Machado wrote of your second journey,
There is no road walker, you make the road
by walking. By walking you make the road,
and when you look backward you see the path

that you never will step on again.
And when you've crossed the fields fired
with wild flowers, you do not look back
but come to an eddy and there find,

held over the swirling water, a temple
where your first woman of this flesh
lights candles in her window at sundown.
Does she await your arrival? The cliffs

so steep here, the wind so like her
fierce breathing, so close to your own
breathing. Now you stand above the shore
on these green mountains, the way back overgrown.

The guards awaken but no longer
have the will to pursue you. You reside
in the house of women, where the Poets
are free to come and go. Li Po counsels,

*There is another heaven and earth
beyond the world of men.* At sunset you walk
to the water's edge. The chilly waves
collapse at your feet and above a woman

sets a table for two, a table where bread
is not of the body but warm precursor
to the evening meal—and wine no longer
the body's life fluid but something of the earth

given back, something deeply red, something
pleasant to pour into a terra-cotta cup
and simply drink for the pure pleasure
of sharing one thing with another.

THAW

We wondered where the headlands were,
if we were meant to follow one
of the various rivulets north, back up

through rock-base and bird-perch,
to come upon a gentle pasture,
a grassy breach above rock

and the rook's nest, beyond the tight,
speedy passage of water gaining
momentum in the thaw and flow, detachment

of recent winter—seasonal loosening,
distilled fish rising
to surface bait, to hook and eye

of the wanderer, eye of the sun, opaque
lunar tooth. And down, the water gravity-
driven, so long bestilled, winter-gripped,

frozen to place and now in the gradual
heat-rise filing down again
the ancient river-groove—down river-seam,

rock-gouge along moss-bank. The melt
now at headland pasture, so long under
white, cow-grass and base-wood bud firing

the prebank sprawl settling into early spring,
the drape and lank of a sultry summer,
the languid opening, the delicate twigs

of Swedenborg's angels exploding to blossom
as the truth played the obvious
and we took the moment to think back.

We were wandering there and I remembered
(or was it you who said it?), it was a path
we pursued, the two of us blinded by scent—

but it might merely have been casual destination,
to be among what opened. What did we call it?
The river-run and wild thyme. The shore-chive.

Ebb and flow.

REAL ESTATE

No stream ran through the twenty-seven acres,
  but the approach had at every turn
    the listed twenty-foot boulders, and at the top

a view looking north over the peaks
  enclosing the summer-dressed valley.
    The house was Adirondack-style and gothic,

the fronting wood damp. Two apricot trees guarded the entryway,
  trees once planted in barrels, now burst through,
    plunging back to true earth, wearing the rotting containers

like bracelets. The owners died a decade ago
  but the kitchen had been left as if they'd gone to the store
    and were about to return. A fork set casually on a blue dish,

a few spoons placed in a glass, empty now but for the residue
  of something coating the spoon tips. I tried to imagine
    spending a night here and looked back to the door,

as if I might otherwise forget the way out.
  The original hardware hung everywhere —
    butterfly hinges, wormwood doorstops and copper doorknobs —

the plumbing built and enameled in the twenties.
  The Reverend Wolf and his wife must have sat for hours
    at the green Formica table, waiting for their weak tea

to brew. They must have discussed something common —
  of that last day or the next, of the town or the neighbors.
    But the room issued a substance conspiratorial and dark,

and the hallway out of the kitchen, which I never entered,
  promised something peculiar and unpleasant—like uncommon animals
    allowed to wander at night through the rooms upstairs.

It was a dark day at the Wolfs' this sunny midsummer day
  in the valley. I thought of the black earth outside
    that held these people in their hollow, dugout plot

somewhere at the back of the property.
  For some reason I reached over and turned on
    the faucet in the unintentionally marbled sink.

The water ran clear and very cold up through the earth,
  this piece of earth where the owners had turned
    from the life that's my estate to a rotting house of spare remains.

INFESTATION

Even insects have histories,
but they're not interesting histories.
— LORD ALFRED WHITEHEAD

Soberly the exterminator says,
      Dampness brings spiders in,
   through windows, under doors, on the air . . .

I don't mind wildlife,
      but at night when the new dark
               turns my body into the blind prey
      of what requires no light
     to feed, forage, and generally access
                  their tranquilized estate—
it's impossible to relax,
         to fall into the gentle sleep
    that's said to be indispensable
         for cerebral stability.

I don't imagine they perpetrate real damage—
      the truth is I simply prefer sleeping alone,
   no middle-of-the-night touching,
           no erratic feet scurrying
    from one blood point to another.
And if dampness
     is what they're after then I'm their quarry, it's me
      they find damply aglaze in the hot room I inherit—
   neither fan nor gentle breeze for reprieve,
              just this body
     a slick in the dark, damp feeding ground,
    dish for the invisible,

   these white sheets the plate
      upon which they take their evening meal.

ALL CITY

He was all city, but not in sports—
something a little different,
a true poet of the urban predicament,

certainly nothing approaching *natural*.
It was a night lit by a moon nearly full
and there was a great deal of sand,

a beach in fact on a fashionable island.
A critic concealed between waves
called back to the beach,

Don't even think about a nature poem! So far
had his reputation taken him from anything
rustic. He may have been wonder struck, seeing

so many stars at once, so close—
the cool, thick Atlantic tide
rushing up and over his two-tone wingtips.

And then out of nowhere he amazed his hosts,
slipping out of his well-pressed clothes
and into the gentle slap

of minor surf, dunking his head into the water,
floating on his back nearly ecstatic
looking up at the lunar disk—aqueous, drifting.

CINEMA VERITÉ

In the cinema verité of the sixties the beautiful
        protagonists always came so close,
so close to the everlasting

        sunset they were so desperately scripted
to ride into. And we, passive onlookers,
        pressed forward in our collective seats

and rooted for them, individually
        and collectively. In the end it went poorly
for those we cheered. As if in imitation

        art led us down its artificial path,
every branch blossoming, the thyme walks
        kicking up the herbal scent, the insects insane

for the goodwill so well distributed.
        Good news has the metabolism of a hummingbird,
its instrument not long attuned to this world.

        Bad news won't extend the prognosis, but time
slows down at its intervention.
        The news, because it's finite, is never good

for long. But when the sun rises over the hills,
        the colored scents of August and the autumnal months
find current and pass on the air. We're okay.

It's the most we can expect, the temperature
of objects in various weathers, the satisfaction
        of things fitting together, whether in the hand

or mind. We're happy to sit down properly attired
        to a meal at day's end, knowing the days
are numbered but the evening is long.

DANCE

The line of girls anathema,
pale summer dresses, conspicuous makeup,
no single expression of welcome:

I sit behind you in math class,
he says to the invited
in every moment of wordlessness.

Want to dance? Sure it's lonely
not dancing. Or is his loneliness
not unlike the loneliness of those unattended?—

to ask and be turned back
no worse than not asked at all?
Want to dance? He's well liked

by family and friends, and he has dreams
that take him beyond this gym,
less dance hall than basketball court,

beyond rock-and-roll to something future.
But he's asking only to *dance.*
An invitation to enter the floor,

nothing permanent, nothing personal
beyond a few steps to the beat he draws
from the history of rock-and-roll.

Isn't the breath of dancing girls ginger?
Standing on guard they both wait and don't wait.
The evening moves on the heat of the rhythm.

Want to dance? is what he must remember,
nothing more. Hand in her hand,
hand on her hip through the conspicuous beat

should they dance—*Do you want to?*—
down the line of girls. He sees their darkened eyes,
their legs moving already. *Dance?*

CARELESS PERFECTION

According to Lin Yutang,
both Po Chuyi and Su Tungp'o
"desperately admired" Tao Yuanming,

a poet of nature who wrote a single love poem,
a poem thought by Chinese dilettantes to be
the one "blemish in a white jade."

Can a poet be faulted for calling a woman
"carelessly perfect in beauty"?
He chose to long for her by envying

the candle that glowed upon her
beautiful face, the shadow
that followed in her every move.

Yet the nature poet Tao Yuanming, at home
with the sudden turning of seasons,
now feared the shadow in darkness,

a discarded fan that once stirred her hair,
feared the candle at dawn. At last believed
that for beauty he had lived in vain.

NATURE LOVER'S LAMENT

They want only to look at it.
Or they need to think about it
And discover they want to know it
That's it—
Just know it.
They ask nothing more from it.
And in this way believe they possess it.
They give up what they have for it,
Even if it
Comes to leaving each other for it.
They look at it,
They talk about it,
They even surrender to it.
But when the moment comes, they refuse to *touch* it.

HUNGRY AS DOGS

You write only of the night? she writes
from one of her outposts. At such a distance
she becomes memory and reminder, a woman I knew
threaded out now so far
only letters and silhouette remain,
her face and hair *at night,* the edges
set by the backlight of whatever wedge of moon
hovered in the window, the white
curtains drawn back to allow the flow
of any available wind that happened to be about
inside. I knew her in the darkest hours,
soundless, murky—the personal hours,
private and slow, the sweetest hours.

Remember that night?
We went outside to the grass
and spread the blanket to our bed.
There was a chill in the air, it must have been
late summer. The trees,
beginning to dry, were noisy on the wind.
We brought with us the dinner we forgot to eat,
something fried and a delicacy
from the sea on damp toast,
other things but abandoned now
by memory. It was the last night, no?
Everything we wore (even our skin) was white—
"a midnight picnic in white,"
we said, and laughed,
transported there on the lawn.
We were famished, wasn't that why we went out?
Hungry as dogs.

A PLACE TO EAT

Do you remember driving south looking for a place to eat? Coming upon a shack on a lagoon that fried fish and chips? They made us wait so we walked out onto the tiny pier that penetrated the small body of water, murky and unfriendly. It was tropical America, overgrown with a vegetation that might have been invented that morning, muscular, definite, dogged in sunlight trope. When we reached the end of the pier we turned back to find the railing suddenly crawling with spiders the size of your woman's fist. It was as if they'd come out just as the sun fell through the waterline to feed, as if this pier were a web and we hopelessly in it. We'd come for romance, to patch up something old—a little southern sentimentality: the long drive through the damp heat of afternoon, a meal at twilight at the end of the road, the trip back north through a starlit night. The spiders might have been mechanical, their movement orchestrated, each group of legs so completely in synch, so completely simultaneous. We walked back keeping to the middle of the pier looking straight to the end. The fried red fish was light and crisp, the beer surprisingly cold. We held hands momentarily but the meal demanded their complete attention. Back in the car we saw a string of lights come on along the rails of the pier, the green simmering water of the lagoon a few degrees from a low boil. The faint scent of oil hovered in the car, the evening blew in through the open windows. It was a great meal. Do you remember what came next? Our hands dead at arms' length? How the headlights finally found the broken white rule running north?

DESPERADOS

We were desperate. No, we were beyond desperation.
We were beside ourselves. At wit's end.
We said we could slip outside, that was it.
Get in the car and just keep on driving. Never look back.
No second thoughts. No chance of posing as salt.

But they'd find us, you said. *They'd bring us back
and it would begin again.* We could start a new life.
We could begin again, trying the something new.
The road ahead again untrod, winding beyond the next curve
with speed and assurance. Did I say we were desperate?

The lightning took over and revealed the night.
The landscape looked altered—rocks and trees
no longer where they had been hours before.
We hadn't made a move, but we were desperate.
Desperate still—oh, desperate beyond description.

But they'd find us, you said. *They'd bring us back.*
We said we could slip outside, that was it.
Never look back. No second thoughts.
We were desperate. At wit's end. Beside ourselves.
The landscape looked altered, beyond description.

We could begin again. Something new.
The landscape looked altered. Never look back.
Did I say desperate to try something new?
A new life? The road ahead untrod, winding beyond.
We hadn't made a move—just kept on driving.

ABIDING MEMENTO

Always going back there
hilltown dinners

tiny yellow Fiat
tracing acres of *rubesco*

growing to maturity
in the amazing pre-autumnal heat

bats haunting the basement
scorpions affixed to stucco walls

cold nights the fireplace blasting
flame like a domestic kiln

sunken bathtub in the bedroom
dribble of the morning shower

glass of chilled Lungarotti at midnight
among stars and impassioned mosquitoes

how even at that moment it was
this memory in time flowing back

FIRST FEVER

Here's a fevered child
bedded down between us.
Here's a child tossing
through the dark hours,
hours when the outcome
must *always* remain
uncertain.
Here we are beside her,
the sleepless, listening
for breath unit and heartbeat,
physiology's simple ongoingness,
an example of pattern,
commonplace rhythm,
certain rise, chronic fall.
I touch the matted hair,
the little girl's damp body.
Her unsteady eyes have no
context, her hoarse voice
no words for what passes
through her.
We haven't come so far,
our race, who can't
diminish this in one child
under the finger of so minor
a demon. So, what's outer
space when pain resides
in the face of the little
loved ones who look to us
to free them? At this hour
we can't tell them what
they will in a different hour

know for themselves. The air
tonight is motionless,
and the heat settled
in her palms and soles.
We plant in her
the glass instrument
because we need to know
what heat inhabits
this body placed now
in our custody.
The night posts no hour,
the dark — cotton blotting
out the world beyond us.
Who's delirious? A film of sweat
covers each of us. Of course
it's not life-threatening,
but this is about impermanence,
not first fever, her first brush
(cleaned, scented, softly combed)
with mortality. She's unaware
of elements less friendly
than these two fevered faces now,
looking deeply for her,
the child held today
in our sustaining custody, high
above the darkening, faced
toward the cooling dawn.

DAUGHTER & CHAIR

It's a sunny day in the middle of the year.
   My daughter in a new white dress
      suns herself in a very bright green beach chair.

She's too young to sit there for long,
   just long enough to pursue a dream,
      a single longing: a sweet, a new toy.

The sun is steady, late afternoon. She's an only child
   and we worry she's lonely, even when dressed up
      and dreaming. If we ask her she pretends not to hear

and pulls at her reddish hair, looking off.
   If we ask again she'll say, *Yes, lonesome.*
      There's only the one sun and it shines in her eyes.

CARNIVAL FOOD

On two lines by John Ashbery

It was great to see you the other day
at the carnival. Our enchiladas were delicious,

the turtles in their glass bowls so cheerfully
colored, although their soup would lack true depth.

I was going to bring my daughter of four years to see
the trick chickens but she came into my room

this morning to tell me she was running
a temperature of 9.6 [sic], too sick to leave her bed.

How would I have explained you to her? You shouldn't
be the Fat Woman, and the tricks you finally mastered

wouldn't really work here. Can you ride a horse?
Grow jumbo squash? Has that green chili of yours improved

disproportionately? I tried another beef enchilada—
it was amazing, not too spicy. I hope you had one.

You looked terrific in the livestock tent,
the cast of your skin that of blue ribbon

melon. I hadn't realized till I saw you
the other day that I had forgotten, well, *you*—

or *us*. Why didn't you call? What a lonely
green wilderness you left me to wander in.

But my god you were beautiful. A vegetarian, right?
It comes back to me. Forget those brilliant enchiladas.

CARNIVAL MOOD

But my god you were beautiful. A vegetarian, right?
It comes back to me. Forget those brilliant enchiladas

I offered you one after another outside the 4-H tent.
Can you ever forgive me for suggesting meat?

What's a memory lapse compared to true history?
It comes back to me, those sweet teeth of yours.

My daughter understands sweets. Yesterday while playing
with the unlit barbecue she glanced over at me and said,

My tooth tells me when I need a Mint Milano
(didn't you have some mechanism like that?),

but I had forgot to buy them at the Pennington Shop Rite.
Guess you shopped wrong, she reprimanded, her budding

sense of humor only just approaching blossom.
What about protein? Isn't that a danger for your people?

Really, it was great seeing you after so long.
We haven't changed in so many essential ways—

sure, gravity's had its way with us
and there's an accumulation here and there—

but there we were, walking around the exhibits on our own.
Could you believe the clothes they wear for the carnival?

I suppose zucchini fritters rival corn dogs,
but if you have to think about this before finding a line

to stand in, why bother eating at all? My daughter says,
if pressed about her appetite, *When I chew my brain hurts.*

Who cares if you prefer grass and flowers to flesh?
"Carnival rhetorical," no? On display two heads or one totally massive.

Submit your questions in the form of an open hand
to the palmist in her tent. Everything's a matter

of degree: meat, my sweet memory, more vegetable than mineral.
Or as my daughter queried, *Which is higher—space or heaven?*

TATTOO

Did you see a cockatoo? I ask.
A white bird with colored head and tail?

Lily, too, she says, her finger
singling out a particular infinity above.

I pin the decal to her forearm
with a little water and a damp cloth.

Cocka-tattoo, she says, and smiles,
below pun but above the literal.

Lily, too! she demands, which means only
there's another location she can imagine

requires a little water, dampness
of the rag and the raiment of *cockatoo.*

The white bird sits on her arm, a solitary
bird more colorful for its pale backdrop.

And beneath its perch in the unclouded weather
the vestal river-blood threads the estuaries

of a body in bud, a body in the dim hours
of morning about to call for *cocka-tattoo.*

She awakens in the shadow of her fingers waving
in the predawn subliminal mind, a body open,

pliable, longing in trope for more tattoo.
Where's Lily's white bird? I ask.

Lily's white bird tattoo, Lily's cocka-tattoo?
Good-bye, Daddy, she adds in so early the hour,

by which she means the time's come for me to find
new postage, replacement for that paling bird

washed and worn into infinity by childish devotion
to what's here now. A bird of restrained flight.

A BAD YEAR

We call it a bad year,
diseases of the blood,
fragile organs, the bone gone awry—
not even the face left simply to age.

Things have to change, we can't go on like this!

one of us says over Chambolle-Musigny and beef
cooked beyond medium to avoid
(as the waiter puts it) *E. coli* lawsuits.
But the truth is we subscribe to the color
and texture of our meat, its total desiccation,
because somehow we've gotten used to all this.

We don't have to accept life pitched this way,

one of us says at the funeral of a distant friend.
We admit to each other much later, after consuming
a quantity of cancer-producing but vintage liquid
that life is not what once it seemed to be:
an endless tangle of plans—what to do,
who to see, where to go, how to get there. . . .

What a year it's been for those around us,

we say at the wedding of a friend
(his fifth) (a woman some of us dated).

Oh, it's just a bad year,

we say, sitting around after a minor meal.
A bad year. What of the lives we once lived?
lives that sprawled
before us like summers that lasted,
vacations that promised and delivered—
those simple, unencumbered "good times"?
when we looked into the future,
putting into gear a new car with a full tank.

What's yet to come? It can't get much worse!

we say upon waking to no one in particular—
or to the morning sun, the reflection in the sheets—
with a cheerfulness that seems false even in solitude.
We check with an index finger the body's geography
for mountains and molehills, and time goes by.

The sky takes on western colors. There's no second coming
and the end—can't we feel it in what's left
of our bones?—is just a stone's throw away.

HERE AT FIFTY

The checklist at dawn
gets longer,

you turn over (if you can),
test hip, knee and elbow —

the joints that once turned
unconsciously like the parts

of new machinery, never
giving away their complexity.

You're pleased to see a new day
breaking over the old,

whatever the local weather.
Long-term plans

mature like short-term
Treasury bills, and summers,

once half a lifetime,
clap like long weekends.

Call it what you like,
but on damp mornings

you get the idea — refusals
of the body politic,

the soul languidly
turning Republican.

Small things
put you in jeopardy,

like crossing the street
or rising too quickly

after a lingering meal.
Don't generalize

the gradual stiffening
that approaches unobserved

and arrives like a hammer,
like puberty taking up

residence, taking control.
No need to look back

over your shoulder (even if you can).
No need to anticipate

what's obvious if uninvited:
the unavoidable, the uninhabitable.

The final midpoint, the last step,
the infinite standstill.

DIRECTION

Along the way there are signs, nothing
obvious, small things laid
as if randomly but reasonably along the way.

Which is the way forward, which
the way back to those first useless
instruments of direction?

I can see from where I stand the diving birds
of this inland waterway, small surface fish
boiling in the presunset heat hunting
the hovering insects skittering the minor ripples—

each moving toward a destination unlike mine
because my path is not destined,
although the one direction now is forward.

Miles of landscape, twigs, branches,
stones and flattened leafage point out
one way or another, the infinity of one location.

Ahead the countless amber caps of kelp
listing toward the shore on the horizon,
the limitless ocean passing over the many bones.

RUSTED TIN

What washes up, what's left behind, what's
forgotten, donated, by chance discarded —
it begins with something shining

in an unencumbered light — luster
and glow, gift and polish,
bright, smooth and new.

It slows down, comes to an end,
runs out. Which is to say,
becomes *familiar,* in the jargon of cliché

taken for granted — like love that lasts,
like good wine drunk without cessation,
like all that is steady, resistant to change.

The news is old: giving up, taking back —
accepting what rolls in, what befalls our beach,
as it were. Our beach. *Our* place.

What drifts here we inherit. Flotsam,
indistinct, valuable — the encrusted,
the laid bare. Here at our feet.

Here at our feet — inching toward us on
a seasoned tide, the random offering riding in,
bearing unbidden but beautiful gifts.

THE ETERNAL LIGHT OF TALK

That's one way to look at it, I thought,
without naming it, leaving the thing
unnamed, without definition—still,
just beyond, breathing but silently.

Well, he would have thought of it that way
too. A passing on of language, like the gift
of one of his beloved oxymorons, like
famous poet or *living will* or *sure thing,*

or a bottle of his favorite bargain Bordeaux
to accompany one of his famously elaborate meals
compiled of unlikely ingredients—
like his palette of language.

Or late into the evening, to himself,
it might have been a passing *through*
language to the other side, a landscape
no longer requiring hip and knee for transport.

And over there if there's *foie gras* he's found it,
and when he found it he found a way
to import the right Chardonnay to keep it company.
I never met a sweetbread I didn't love, he would say

sipping slyly on a rare, woody white isolated
on a sudden mission to the West Coast.
He had a life he kept even from himself.
I never heard him utter an interrogative.

Why be surprised by the unknown?
We made it a point to toast the life
we seemed to be leading
wherever we found ourselves.

Who else would so intuitively name a cat Velcro?
Or love Mingus and Donizetti with equal vigor?
The vocabulary for solace is impoverished.
To be sure, his was a living will.

IN SEASON

The game birds you like to pursue await
disagreeable weather.
Is it right to hunt birds before

the vegetation turns against green?
I don't like holding guns
but I've looked through the "Victory" at game

and pulled the trigger.
Bang?
It's such a small town you call home.

If there's a stream anywhere nearby
trout's a regular at your table:
a fist of lemon, a few thimbles

of imported oil, seasonings
and a grill oiled and hot enough
to crisscross-brand the fresh fish flesh.

We invoke private boats crossing
the Channel, 19th-century picnics
on a simple white sheet,

a pale, sweetish white from the Rhine,
probably dark bread and Alsatian Muenster,
some bright, ripe fruit from the coast

with those we don't truly care most about.
We aim to keep it simple:
long anticipation,

an excited greeting,
a slow, melancholy, but necessary
parting . . .

We are as good as our word,
our promise deep. Oh yes,
this life argues against chance romance,

against the Romantic Life,
against giving over to body reflex.
Argue: the sexual trope the trope

of affection. What was that? *In season,* we say.
The weather, we say of our private cycles—
finite diversion the art of this world.

NEW STRANGERS

Here's to you!—to you
on the other side of the table.
Your eyes give you away, dark,
focused, a color
not from around here, or
how you push back
your thick, untangled hair.

Let's talk. The sky is bristling
with constellations holding
our future. Here's to you!—
three or four vowel-filled syllables
to your name, a brief music
awakening in the predawn hours,
a chant, reference and query.

Neglect the unintentional
filling like ticks in late spring,
how the social kindles privacy—
what you might say!
Let's talk. Your eyes, they ignite
with the private vision. Your hands
play the air to a music not our own.

Tell me about you again.
It's so easy to forget
when your mind's adrift on a river
of its own. The shore flows by
so quickly. Do you understand?
Strangers. Isn't it amazing
they've been here? And always so familiar.

BEAUTY & RESTRAINT

We decided to make nothing definite.
We decided it was in the nature of things
to change, in the morning
best to leave through different doors.

What did we say about the future?
A bullet fired into the air
but never found is how we expressed it,
expressed our feelings about the future.

It's paradise out there—
the approach of evening, the sun setting
over no landscape in particular,
the air shot with salt, fragrant with a breeze

climbing the hillside terraced to the sea
with flowers. And to the east,
through louvered windows, unforgettable vistas
best left undescribed.

The evening is upon us, the sun's paint
a blood-orange not seen since the Renaissance,
the air of possibility palpable,
momentarily definite here in twilight paradise.

But no matter how far into the sunset
we might willingly ride, we understand how
even the sun, hovering in this paradise,
eventually goes down.

LATE

It is the harsh, rude sound of a man leaving—
first the light catching in one of the mirrors,
then darkness closing back over the room.
Then the sound of the door returning to its latch.

She lies below the single cotton sheet, her hands
inattentive at her sides, her hair spiked with heat,
her cheap chemise climbing back down her hips
with the gauzy design of sleep beginning its pull.

She allows the stars to reappear at the window
while the wind works the trees into a sound
almost male. And beyond—the lost or inaudible
repetition of walking shoes, moving with intent.

MEASURES SHE HAS TAKEN

The cruelties of Africa cloud the nails
of her fingers as they tour
the side of her amazing face.

She moves to a sexual music, played
with dexterity but single fingered,
with languid candor.

As a child her native tongue
was scent, vegetal, cleaving
to color alone, one surface, clean.

She is home to such cruelties,
blades rising from uncommon ground,
their edges rubbed with dulling towels.

Her house deforms such acts
paling the land, the foliage
of roadside, the choked headlines.

Lost are the ingenuous, clipped zeal
of the sexual wash, a world
beyond the pellucid. The solitary trade.

She won't take on strangers.
At the edge of the window find now
a little open ocean, the sun afloat on Orient.

HØEG'S ISLAND

She lived on an island connected to an island by a bridge, a wooden bridge that could breathe with the weather — expand, pull back, accommodate the seasons: deep summer to arctic freeze. The first time he saw her it was late summer, in a pale green dress without shoes, standing in the grass off to the side of one of the island's sandy roads. Her hair like the hair of the women of this island was pale, the color of the island light, of the sandy roads, and hung straight around the pale almond of her face. The meeting was momentary but definite, she had said something — to him? — that was caught by a gust of wind and dispersed. Then they moved away, he across the bridge to the island where he visited friends, she remaining on the island where she lived. When they met again she told him in the voice of a young girl that she had never been off her island, never crossed the breathing bridge to the sister island coupled to it. And that was the last time he saw her until he found her in a dream, running across the bridge through a thick fog, barefoot, wearing a lime-green dress. Her pale hair flowed behind her, her speed amazing to him. He followed her to a small harbor and when he reached the end of the pier, he saw that the fog had cleared. She was on water turned jade in the moonlight, on a boat set with flaxen sails. Her hair, like the sails pulling her away, moved on the wind. When she was gone he returned to the bridge, the foliage in the clarity of the full moon turning from the easy greens of early fall to the suggestive saffrons of transition. What had she said the day they met? Her words, visible it seemed in his dream as birds of indeterminate color, flew at an angle into the rising sun — forms punctuating the language of what lay ahead.

AIR, '56

I see the lives of neighbors mapped and marred
like all the wars ahead. . . .
— WELDON KEES

Across the way a phonograph scratches out "Ja-Da."
A passing car—pale green and milky white—
spills out something more recent with a quicker beat.
The light slips into something informal.

There's the scent of back-to-school, leafage
suffering in piles, going up in thin shafts
of smoke. A restrictive, brownish air, sweet
and acrid, brooding and optimistic—

the air of vacation dispersed.
Down the street:
Sweeney will disappear in Asia.
Tierney a year from the iron lung.

The unnamed, contemporary tune a strike
on the hit parade, released on the leafy air.
It could have been Buddy de Franco on the clarinet,
he made "Ja-Da" sound hollow, like an autumnal chill,

lonely, something to resolve in the company
of those lived among—trusted and well loved.
It rose down the way, chatty and cool,
melody climbing the coolish, friendly air.

BUENA VISTA SOCIAL CLUB

Their old, pale green Pontiac cleaned up
and parked outside
the Buena Vista Social Club.
And inside the musicians
of the other Cuba—Ruben Gonzalez
and Eliades Ochoa, Ibrahim Ferrer
and Compay Segundo—brought out
like antique instruments
for the hip gringo musician.

And the music—trumpets
placed back just far enough from the singers
to make the sound that other Cuba.

They wore white berets and white buck shoes,
striped shirts and brown chino trousers—the beat was up-
beat, the mood the mood of reunion, a reunion
of melody and rhythm: the stars of *cubano musica*
with Cooder making the boys remember,
bringing them back to it,
like this was it—like this was
just another scorching midsummer night in Havana,
the forty years no longer a thing of the past,
the sun waiting to rise up against the new day.

DINNER FOR TWO

It wasn't an easy address to find, buried in Chinatown, above the dried fish and red chickens, the redolent, the desiccated, the fermented products from the sea. I rang the bell hoping for a table of eight, his reputation such that dinner alone was unthinkable. *Good evening,* I said. *It's just the two of us,* he replied, greeting me. We shared a split of *prosecco* from a town I knew in Lombardy, which started us off well enough. We moved on to something winning from the Kumeu River, a crisp New Zealand white that was a test for us both. When the conversation lagged, but only just, he read a few poems from Hinton's translation of T'ao Ch'ien, which settled us down: *. . . in wine / I touch countless distances . . . I only regret / drinking so often without enough wine.* We sat down to eat, a stewed rabbit marinated five days in Chinese herbs and spices, etc. Asian greens and rice permeated with sesame oil. A perfect meal—execution, balance, taste—but I was most touched by the lengthy preparation that had begun some days earlier. He made our salad in the sink, in a colander, pouring first an aged rice vinegar, then the first-pressed olive oil, pointing out the obvious incompatibility of oil and water. The meal was perfect and the talk, like that between old colleagues, rehashed what had come before, speculated on what remained ahead. When his wife arrived we talked about the book she was working on, a history of pre-Stalinist Russian politics, before I took my leave. Downstairs the Chinese shopkeepers prepared for the new day. There were meat trucks and wagons of vegetables cluttering the streets with volume and scent. I bought something deep-fried and walked home, thinking about the evening. Of course it had been a perfect evening. He could not have been more gracious despite his reputation. I told myself I'd call him and we'd do this again, knowing I probably wouldn't. Not because it wasn't a perfect evening. But perfect evenings are never repeated—and then there are the hazards of comparison, as with all human intercourse. We met again, but at a large event. We agreed that it had been a perfect evening, that we must do it again. I was to call sometime soon. And I will call. Maybe I'll take him up on that tour of the Chinese food stores, to have a look at what only the initiated get to see (he is a man of food well beloved in that neighborhood), maybe even taste something very old and odd and intense. I'd like to do that.

BRAVURA LAMENT

He would tell you the grass this spring was a pale
imitation of the deep lushness of the year gone by.

He would say the notes from the reed of Charlie Parker
stirred him to a longing no longer soluble,

a kind of dampness leaving him, for days at a time,
inconsolable. Although he would not be remembered

as a brave man, those who knew him well would say
what he lived at the end was akin to bravura lament.

Of the constellations that summer he would locate
only the brightly conspicuous stars of Ursa Major,

his head back, his eyes vacant but focused light-years
down that starry road, his grizzled mouth slack

and mindless, like a turkey's in a downpour swiveled up,
drowning while showered by the fluid blow of keen insight.

FORESEEABLE FUTURES

We would have found Powell in Paris
had we been there in the sixties,
a damp club off Saint-Germain, hot,
filled with the blue smoke of Gauloise
and the female scents of jasmine and champac.

The small, round tables—wobbly
against our knees—balanced milky glasses
of *petite bordeaux.* And onstage
Bud at the keyboard, head down, Pierre
Michelot on bass, Kenny Clarke alive on drums.

The other day your son sent me
the woodcut of a musician you used
on the cover of one of your books.
Foreseeable Futures. I wonder
if you saw yours. The summer we rented a house

in Umbria it seemed we'd live for a long time.
It was certainly our intention,
drinking *rubesco* on the little balcony
watching the fields across the way.
It was better living without signs,

to live as if we'd live forever,
that there'd be time for Powell in Paris,
a few meals in the best bistros,
well-prepared organ meats that had such a pull
on you. And after the meal the music,

the smooth, seamless jazz out of the smoky dark,
a little talk about life between sets,
the wine setting in, the new day not so far away.
We could have done this in a foreseeable future.
We could have found our way to the music.

HOMAGE TO N.

after Chekhov

She is the most beautiful woman in Moscow,
young, petulant, unpredictable,
proud, and quite wise—a complete mystery to him.
N. understands in general how much there is
yet to grasp—about his young wife
and his life in the most general sense.
Yet he fails to take to heart the heartfelt advice
his father offers on the eve of his marriage:
If loneliness is what you fear, marriage isn't for you.
Their first night together she brings him a chilled bottle
of mineral water with a preserved cherry at the bottom,
which they share, talking, touching each other
until first light brings the hotel to life,
and they drift deeply into sleep.
During the first years of their marriage,
N. goes nightly to see his young wife onstage.
They are so close in these days that when she delivers
a particularly winning line, he must summon restraint,
must somehow resist a powerful urge to stand up, turn,
and bow to the audience.

*

N. is again enraged by his wife,
an actress inflated with an ambition
fettered to a modest talent.
To cool down
he calls on two acquaintances
the evening of her opening.
The first to secure savage reviews
in the morning papers,

and then on to her current lover
to borrow money to stage his new play
he's decided to call *The Power of Harmonies.*

*

N. has always loved A.—
from their days in school,
their summers at the lake—
her long dark hair gathered
in a swirl atop her head
even as a young girl.
At twenty she marries Y.
and moves to an outlying district
of Taganrog, where they set up house:
a whitewashed fence, a flock of cats,
they plant bright flowers
that spring forth each April.

A few years later
A. comes to N. and on his shoulder
begins to cry—she needs to talk,
to explain something important to her.
N. believes he will hear the sadness
of her life with Y., of her long-denied
feelings for N., harbored
for so endless a time.
She wipes her pretty eyes
on the wide, colorful scarf
wrapped around her shoulders,
her face alive, intense.
A. begins the intricate and animated story
of her love for D.

*

N. has been plagued during the holiday season
with long nights of insomnia and bad dreams.
His dreams remain autobiographical, that is,
no product of the imagination. The weather's
been crisp, what they call seasonable,
and his diet has remained stable: dried fish
in the morning with eggs, greens at midday,
a little meat, well-cooked, potatoes and fried bread
at dinner. But the dreams continue nightly
through the final march of days toward Christmas.
He is short with his family, distracted by the wind
or news in the papers from Moscow. What is it?
Christmas Eve he awakes to a wind lashing the pines
outside the house, from a dream in which his wife
lay with her legs cut off below the knees
and he, dressed in a white cossack, nursed her back
with the sole intention of saving his own dark soul.

*

Not a day goes by when N. doesn't pour himself
a glass of cold milk, which he takes into his study,
sits in his chair and places the glass on his work table.
At the window he traps a plump spring fly
and carries it cupped in his hands
to the table, where he drops it into the milk.
He returns to his chair and rings, always with an air
of distraction, the silver bell that will summon
the butler who has served him for thirty years.
What's that? he asks of the old servant.

*

After his marriage ends N. seems to his closest friends
inconsolable—which is a mystery, really.
He has complained of her for years, railed at her over dinner,

constantly sought out the company of younger women—
as he would put it, to inspire his work in the theater
as well as his fiction. And then one day he meets
S. in a lower-class bar in Zolotonosha Street.
She's just shy of fifty, out of N.'s usual range,
but they take up with each other, a liaison that lasts
only a few months. When it ends shortly before Christmas,
N. swings into a more jovial mood. The following spring
he publishes a well-received collection of ghost tales.

*

N. is in love. He's forty, she's seventeen.
The weather no longer dictates the day.
Clouds, sun, it's all the same to N.
She's a girl from a neighboring village
who agrees to marriage. It's a bright day,
their friends and family assemble, rings
are exchanged. After the marriage
they unlock the door to their new cottage,
place a few birch logs in the fireplace
and in the dark undress, meet under the woolen
blanket spread over the bed. Is this his happiest
moment? Her tears make stars of the fledgling
firelight, her sad hair a shadow between them.
Her impasse is agony for him—midnight, a fog
on the air, the temperature going down. What's left
to say, her love youthful miscalculation, the moment
annulled, their life together yawning but briefly ahead,
not much beyond the new day. He lifts the sheets, steps down
into his wolfskin slippers. He finds a blanket
and goes off to sleep in a room at the back of the house.

*

N. tells his students the first day of classes,
In the long run truth will triumph,
which he knows to be untrue. It's his private nod,
his way of sharing a few of life's hard knocks—to live
behind the belief of a higher order,
yet knowing to expect the worst.

*

The snow this winter has been heavier
than N. can remember. Since early fall
he's been hounded by one illness after another.
He's come to his country house to recover.
The wind off the lake is relentless,
hammers at his bedroom shutters
where he sits with a blanket across his knees
reading his favorite novels
from the 18th century. Suddenly N. hears
steps on the front porch, and then a light,
rapid knocking at the door. He pulls back
the curtain at the window and sees a young woman
standing in the cold with a pale, linen suitcase.
He goes down the hall and opens the door.
She tells him she arrived on the afternoon train from Moscow
and walked the seven miles to N.'s house
to look after the invalid. He fears her earnestness,
the intensity that betrays her youthful eyes.
He tells her there must be some mistake.
But no invalid lives here, he tells her,
closing the door slightly and pulling back.
The snow seems to be thickening and the light
has drained completely from the afternoon.
The wind howls over the lake, through the pine trees.
N. understands what must be done, but protests.
At last the young woman says that at any rate
she'll stay the night. A day passes, two,

and she goes on living there, keeping up
the house, washing his clothes and sheets,
cooking modestly on the country stove.
But as time goes by her temper becomes unbearable.
Though cured—one might even say enjoying
excellent health—N.'s very existence
has been poisoned. One night he writes
in the journal he keeps on his bedside table,
The sun shines, but in my soul darkness reigns.

ACKNOWLEDGMENTS

BEST AMERICAN POETRY: "Her Body"

THE DENVER QUARTERLY: "The New Road"

FIVE POINTS: "After Rumi"

THE GETTYSBURG REVIEW: "Beauty & Restraint"

THE JOURNAL OF NEW JERSEY POETS: "After Rumi"

THE KENYON REVIEW: "Carnival Food," "Carnival Mood," "The Eternal Light of Talk"

THE MISSOURI REVIEW: "Midnight: Triadic Ghazal," "Thaw"

THE NEW ENGLAND REVIEW: "Buena Vista Social Club," "Direction"

THE NEW REPUBLIC: "After the Vigil," "Cinema Verité," "Marriage Poem"

THE NEW YORKER: "Desperados"

THE ONTARIO REVIEW: "Abiding Memento," "Dinner for Two," "Here at Fifty," "Homage to N.," "Hot Tea," "Love Song," "To a Daughter"

PLOUGHSHARES: "Her Body"

POETRY: "Bravura Lament," "Careless Perfection," "Keepers," "Nature Lover's Lament"

PRESS: "Rusted Tin"

THE PRINCETON LIBRARY BULLETIN: "Late"

SALMAGUNDI: "All City," "New Strangers"

SLATE: "Dance," "Fugue," "My Eyes Your Eyes"

THE SOUTHERN REVIEW: "A Bad Year," "Foreseeable Futures," "Infestation," "Moon Over Squibnocket," "Real Estate," "Zeno's Lemur"

TRIQUARTERLY: "Dusk," "Resurrection"

THE YALE REVIEW: "Air, '56"

A Note About the Author

Daniel Halpern was born in Syracuse, New York, and has lived in Los Angeles, Seattle, New York City, Princeton, and Tangier, Morocco. He is the author of eight previous collections of poems, the editorial director of The Ecco Press: an Imprint of HarperCollins, and a recipient of many grants and awards, including fellowships from the Guggenheim Foundation and the National Endowment for the Arts, as well as the 1993 PEN Publisher Citation. For twenty-five years he edited the international literary magazine *Antaeus,* which he founded in Tangier, Morocco, with Paul Bowles. He has taught in the graduate writing program of Columbia University, at The New School for Social Research, and in the writing program of Princeton University.

A Note on the Type

This book was set in Granjon, a type named in compliment to Robert Granjon, a type cutter and printer active in Antwerp, Lyons, Rome, and Paris, from 1523 to 1590. Granjon, the boldest and most original designer of his time, was one of the first to practice the trade of type founder apart from that of printer.

Composed by NK Graphics, Keene, New Hampshire
Printed and bound by Edwards Brothers, Ann Arbor, Michigan
Designed by Peter A. Andersen